SPOTLIGHT ON NATURE
GORILLA

MELISSA GISH

CREATIVE EDUCATION · CREATIVE PAPERBACKS

Published by Creative Education and Creative Paperbacks
P.O. Box 227, Mankato, Minnesota 56002
Creative Education and Creative Paperbacks are imprints of
The Creative Company
www.thecreativecompany.us

Design by Chelsey Luther; production by Colin O'Dea
Art direction by Rita Marshall
Printed in the United States of America

Photographs by Alamy (AF archive, David Cantrille, Eric Gevaert, Nature
Picture Library, Jamie Pham), Getty Images (Lisle Brathwaite/500px Prime,
Ibrahim Suha Derbent/Photodisc, Education Images/Universal Images
Group, Jupiterimages/liquidlibrary, Jacob Maentz/Corbis Documentary,
Francis Miller/The LIFE Picture Collection, HENDRIK SCHMIDT/Stringer/
DPA), iStockphoto (ajball18, Alan_Lagadu, antpkr, aznature, guenterguni,
Max_grpo, Lina Moiseienko, Cheryl Ramalho, Grant Thomas), Minden
Pictures (Suzi Eszterhas, Jabruson/NPL), National Geographic Creative
(CHRIS SCHMID), Shutterstock (LMIMAGES)

Library of Congress Cataloging-in-Publication Data
Names: Gish, Melissa, author.
Title: Gorilla / Melissa Gish.
Series: Spotlight on nature.
Includes index.
Summary: A detailed chronology of developmental milestones drives this life
study of gorillas, including their habitats, physical features, and conservation
measures taken to protect these powerful apes.
Identifiers: ISBN 978-1-64026-339-0 (hardcover) / ISBN 978-1-62832-
871-4 (pbk) / ISBN 978-1-64000-481-8 (eBook)
This title has been submitted for CIP processing under LCCN 2020902479.

First Edition HC 9 8 7 6 5 4 3 2 1
First Edition PBK 9 8 7 6 5 4 3 2 1

CONTENTS

MOUNTAIN GORILLAS

of Bwindi Impenetrable Forest

Bwindi Impenetrable Forest in southwestern Uganda is one of the most heavily forested places on the planet. On Bwindi's mountains, thick vines fill the spaces between soaring sapele mahogany and shorter African cherry trees. Massive eagle ferns cover the ground, along with forest bitterberry and woody tangles of purple flowering mimulopsis. The diversity of edible plants and herbs in Bwindi satisfies even the largest forest residents: mountain gorillas.

It is mid-December, and the dry season has begun. Overnight, the temperature dropped to 48 °F (8.9 °C). A cool mist blanketed the mountainside through the early morning. By midday, the sun has warmed the forest to 80 °F (26.7 °C). A mountain gorilla family relaxes in the shade, munching on fig leaves. Suddenly, one of the females sighs heavily. The other gorillas realize something exciting is about to happen. Soon they will have a new family member.

CLOSE-UP

Scent signals

Gorillas produce body odors unique to the in-dividual. These scents are used to identify each other in the dense forest. Smells also change to indicate emotions such as anger, fear, or love.

CHAPTER ONE

LIFE BEGINS

Gorillas belong to the group of mammals called primates. These are animals with highly developed brains and gripping hands. Gorillas and their closest relatives—chimpanzees, orangutans, and humans—are great apes. These primates have the largest brains. Monkeys and prosimians are also primates. They have tails, snouts, and smaller brains. All apes and most other primates have five toes on each foot and four fingers and a thumb on each hand. This allows them to hold and control objects. Primates have fingernails and toenails instead of claws. Newborns have a weak grip. A primate mother must hold her newborn to her chest so it can feed on the milk she produces. Within a few weeks, it grows strong enough to hang on to its mother's hair by itself.

BWINDI MOUNTAIN GORILLA MILESTONES

DAY (1)

- ▸ Born
- ▸ Covered with sparse fur
- ▸ Weight: 4.5 pounds (2 kg)
- ▸ Height: 10 inches (25.4 cm)

FEATURED FAMILY

Welcome to the World

In Bwindi, the female mountain gorilla rolls onto her back and rubs her belly, which has been growing bigger for eight and a half months. She groans softly. After some effort, she gives birth to a tiny baby. She lifts him tenderly. The mother gorilla slurps fluid from her infant's mouth and nose, clearing his airway. As he takes his first deep breath, he inhales the scent of his mother. Soon, the newborn will learn to recognize scent signals, which indicate anger, distress, or calmness.

The two gorilla species—western and eastern—are divided into four subspecies named for their geographic location. Most gorillas have short black hair, but mountain gorillas have longer hair and thicker body fat suited to their mountainous habitat, where temperatures can drop below freezing. Male gorillas average 5 to 6 feet (1.5–1.8 m) in height and weigh up to 500 pounds (227 kg). Females average just under 5 feet (1.5 m) tall and weigh 155 to 200 pounds (70.3–90.7 kg). Newborns weigh about four and a half pounds (2 kg) and grow quickly.

Mature males between 8 and 11 years old are called blackbacks. Around age 12, white hair begins to grow on their backs from their shoulders to their rumps, and they become

sagittal crest

CLOSE-UP
Sagittal crest

Male gorillas have a bony ridge across the top of their skulls. This is the sagittal crest. It adds power to the gorilla's jaws. A gorilla's bite is nearly eight times stronger than a human's.

8 WEEKS
- Begins crawling on all fours
- Teeth have erupted

10 WEEKS
- Begins eating fruit and leaves
- Weight: 13 pounds (5.9 kg)
- Height: 12.5 inches (31.8 cm)

silverbacks. Gorillas live in troops, or family groups of 5 to 30 members that are run by the strongest silverback. He protects the troop from predators, fathers babies, and resolves conflicts among members. He may have to defend his position from rival silverbacks. Other mature males are ranked below the leading silverback. Females and their immature offspring are below the males, while females without offspring have the lowest status.

CLOSE-UP

Diet

Gorillas eat seeds, leaves, stems, roots, fruits, flowers, bark, and fungi. They also consume grubs and insects that are on these items. Gorillas eat up to 40 pounds (18.1 kg) of vegetation each day.

─── FEATURED FAMILY ───

First Meal

As the sun sets, the temperature starts to drop in the forest. The mother gorilla holds her infant close, covering his body with both hands to keep him warm. The infant's slender fingers curl around strands of her fur. He lets out a soft grunt as his tiny mouth finds milk. The milk provides everything the infant needs. Sugars and fats will strengthen his body, hormones will help him grow, and antibodies will give him the best chance of survival.

Gorillas live in troops of FIVE to THIRTY MEMBERS.

 **3.5 MONTHS**

- Begins riding on mother's back
- Regularly plays with other infants

Long limbs

Gorillas' arms are longer and stronger than their legs. Gorillas can stand and walk upright, but they usually walk using their hind feet and the knuckles of their hands.

CHAPTER TWO
EARLY ADVENTURES

During their first year of life, gorilla infants depend on their mothers for food and protection, but the whole troop participates in the nurturing of infants. Older females teach immature females how to babysit infants. To strengthen infants' muscles, adults gently wrestle with the babies and swing them by their arms and legs. When infants are about 10 weeks old, they start to play with one another. They also begin eating fruit and leaves. As they age, they wrestle and play-fight, chase each other up and down trees, and roll down hills. Such activities strengthen young gorillas' bodies. They learn cooperation skills, too. Juveniles will continue to supplement their diets with their mothers' milk for up to four years. Gorillas digest food slowly. They spend most of the day

(7) MONTHS

- Can easily jump off mother and climb back on
- Eating mostly solid foods
- Weight: 24 pounds (10.9 kg)
- Height: 18 inches (45.7 cm)

(9) MONTHS

- Takes first steps on hind legs
- Climbs trees with ease

— FEATURED FAMILY —

Look Who's Crawling

The Bwindi gorilla infant is now two months old. He has figured out how to crawl. He sets off toward his father, who sits nearby, munching a stalk of bamboo. The infant approaches the massive silverback and reaches out with unsteady fingers. He touches the long, black hair covering the silverback's leg. With a snort, the silverback extends one finger and gently bops the infant on the top of his head. The infant squeals and loses his balance, tipping over and landing on his face in the grass. The silverback tenderly pats the infant's back. One day, this tiny gorilla will be as big and powerful as his father.

When **INFANTS** are about **10 WEEKS** old, they start to **PLAY** with one another.

③ YEARS

- No longer rides on mother's back
- Nests with other juveniles in trees
- Weight: 40 pounds (18.1 kg)
- Height: 32 inches (81.3 cm)

foraging, eating, and napping. A troop may travel about half a mile (0.8 km) each day as it forages. While eating, gorillas sit cross-legged. They often gather and fold food into a kind of sandwich. They bite and shred food with their sharp teeth. Gorillas may eat only certain parts of a food source by tearing or scooping out what they want. They leave the leftovers in a neat pile. Gorillas rarely drink water. They get most of the moisture they need from their food or by licking dew off leaves. After a full day of activity, gorillas sleep 13 to 15 hours at night.

— FEATURED FAMILY —

Give It a Try

In the Bwindi forest, the silverback climbs a tree and knocks a dozen overripe, red fruits to the ground. A juvenile scoops up a fruit and tears into it. The silverback climbs down and races to slap away the fruit. He has not yet given the youngster permission to eat. The infant gorilla watches the drama unfold. Then he sneaks over to the shattered fruit and snatches a tiny piece, shoving this first taste of fruit into his mouth before anyone notices.

④ YEARS

- ▸ No longer drinks mother's milk
- ▸ Witnesses birth of younger sibling
- ▸ Weight: 42 pounds (19.1 kg)
- ▸ Height: 37 inches (94 cm)

CLOSE-UP
Vocalization

Silverbacks scream up-close or hoot from a distance to warn off enemies. Three quick barks ask, "Where are you?" A soft rumble tells others that there is food to share, but loud grunting means "I'm not sharing." Calm gorillas sing, "Mwaaah, hwah, hwah," and playful gorillas chuckle.

CHAPTER THREE
LIFE LESSONS

Young male gorillas learn to lead by watching their troop's silverback, whose commands are followed without hesitation. The lead silverback tells his troop when they should eat, rest, travel, and sleep. During calm periods, he may rumble, grunt, or snort softly to convey reassurance. Silence can also be an important form of communication. When the silverback falls silent and looks intently at his surroundings, he is telling his troop to be quiet and listen—something is out there, and it could be dangerous. When a sudden threat is perceived, he may emit a loud scream. This signal sends youngsters up trees and adults scattering to take cover.

While silverbacks protect their troops by threatening yet rarely fighting, young males still practice the chest-beating and biting skills

8 YEARS

- Leaves mother's company
- Joins adolescent group
- Weight: 75 pounds (34 kg)
- Height: 4.3 feet (1.3 m)

12 YEARS

- Gray hairs appear on back
- Moves up in troop rank to just below head silverback

— FEATURED FAMILY —

This Is How It's Done

As night falls on the Bwindi forest, a leopard steps out of the underbrush. Its gaze lands on the young gorilla, now three years old, climbing a tree to make a nest. In an instant, the silverback jumps to his feet. The juvenile freezes, watching intently. The silverback tears up a handful of grass and throws it. He slaps his chest and angrily screams, "Waaaah!" The leopard disappears. Mimicking this display, the young gorilla slaps a palm against his own chest and squeals. Then he scurries up the tree.

that may prove necessary to lead their own troops. As the youngsters grow up, they play-fight and practice aggressive displays. They stand and beat their chests and throw sticks and dirt. They may charge at each other and even tumble around, nipping arms and legs. When they are 10 to 13 years old, young silverbacks leave their family troops. They either take over an old silverback's troop or gather roaming females who have left their families. Gorillas will not mate with siblings or with unrelated gorillas they have grown up with, whom they consider stepsiblings.

Females also leave their troop when they mature. They begin mating around age 10, typically giving birth once every 4 to 6 years.

<table>
<tr><td>⑬ YEARS</td><td>⑮ YEARS</td></tr>
<tr><td>

▸ Chased away from troop by head silverback
▸ Weight: 420 pounds (191 kg)
▸ Height: 5.2 feet (1.6 m)

</td><td>

▸ Establishes new troop with two females
▸ Mates for the first time
▸ Weight: 480 pounds (218 kg)
▸ Height: 5.5 feet (1.7 m)

</td></tr>
</table>

Females breed only with the silverback leading their troop or his second-in-command (if the silverback allows it). A mother gorilla keeps her offspring close for the first two to three years, carrying the baby on her back as she travels and guarding it as it sleeps. Young females learn nurturing skills by serving as babysitters during the day and nesting with other adolescents in trees at night. Gorillas in captivity may live to be 50, but most wild gorillas live no more than 40 years.

FEATURED FAMILY

Practice Makes Perfect

The Bwindi gorilla is now four years old. His mother holds a new infant on her knee. The curious young gorilla comes closer to his baby sister. He extends a cautious finger toward the infant. She reaches out with a tiny hand and grasps her brother's finger. Though he spent the morning chasing and play-fighting with other adolescents in the troop, he is calm now. One day, when he is a huge silverback, he will have to be this gentle with his own fragile offspring.

GORILLAS RARELY SLEEP IN THE SAME PLACE TWO NIGHTS IN A ROW.

(25) YEARS

(40) YEARS

▸ Troop has grown larger
▸ Father to 12 surviving offspring

▸ End of life

CHAPTER FOUR

GORILLA SPOTTING

Since the mid-20th century, gorilla populations have severely declined. The nations where gorillas live are poor, and many people are desperate for food. This leads to poaching, or illegal killing, of gorillas for bushmeat. Some gorillas have lost hands and feet in illegal snares that hunters set up to catch anything from rabbit-like hyraxes to African buffaloes. Baby gorillas are also captured for the illegal pet trade, which devastates gorilla troops. Another problem is deforestation. This displaces gorillas, leading to their demise.

Three African governments worked together to establish a refuge for mountain gorillas called the Virunga Conservation Area. It includes parts of Bwindi Impenetrable National Park in Uganda, Virunga National Park in Democratic Republic of the Congo, and Volcanoes National Park in Rwanda. In 1978, primate researcher Dian Fossey founded the Digit Fund, which raised money to pay people to patrol mountain gorilla habitat and destroy traps. When Fossey was murdered in 1985 (likely by poachers), the fund was renamed the Dian Fossey Gorilla Fund

International in the United States and the Gorilla Organization in the United Kingdom. Thanks to people who have continued Fossey's work, the population of mountain gorillas has increased from about 300 to nearly 900 in recent decades. While this number is still very low, even modest growth is a good sign.

Cross River gorillas are not so fortunate. They are the world's most endangered great ape. Fewer than 300 mature individuals exist in an area of forest targeted for logging. Slightly smaller than their relatives, male Cross River gorillas average no more than 440 pounds (200 kg). They are extremely shy and difficult to study, which only increases their vulnerability. About 4,000 eastern lowland gorillas and roughly 100,000 western lowland gorillas live in the wild. Despite the higher numbers, these gorillas are also in trouble.

Gorillas share their world with people who struggle with civil war, disease, and poverty. Park rangers tasked with protecting gorillas may be killed by poachers or compelled to work with poachers in order to feed their families. Organizations around the world work with national and local governments in African countries to improve the protection of gorillas. They help develop better land-use plans to curb deforestation and provide education to local communities about the devastating effects of hunting gorillas. The continuation of such large-scale conservation efforts is vital to saving gorillas for future generations.

SNAPSHOTS

Koko was a **western lowland gorilla** who learned to communicate with humans using a version of American Sign Language.

Eastern lowland gorillas, also called Grauer's gorillas, are bigger than other gorilla subspecies, with males weighing up to 500 pounds (227 kg).

Western lowland gorillas inhabit lowland forests from Nigeria to Angola. Their range extends westward to Central African Republic and parts of Democratic Republic of the Congo.

The Digit Fund was named for Digit, Dian Fossey's favorite **mountain gorilla**. He was killed by poachers in 1977.

DIGIT

Michael, a **western lowland gorilla**, was Koko's companion. Koko taught him sign language, which he used to describe his experience with poachers.

Eastern lowland gorillas inhabit rainforests of Democratic Republic of the Congo. They prefer flatter terrain than their mountain-dwelling cousins.

Cross River gorillas, named for their habitat on the Cameroon-Nigeria border, were discovered in 1904 but not closely studied until 1987.

Mountain gorillas are highly social, typically living in tight-knit troops of 6 to 12 members. Rarely, troops may grow to include up to 50 members.

COLO

Born in Ohio's Columbus Zoo in 1956, Colo was the world's first captive-born western lowland gorilla. She lived 60 years, making her the world's oldest known gorilla.

Cross River gorillas typically live in family groups of just four to seven individuals. But troops with as many as 18 members have been recorded.

A **western lowland gorilla** named Snowflake was the world's only known albino, or all-white, gorilla. He lived at Spain's Barcelona Zoo until his death in 2003.

Democratic Republic of the Congo's Kahuzi-Biega National Park is home to the largest population (about 250) of protected **eastern lowland gorillas**.

Binti Jua is a **western lowland gorilla** at Brookfield Zoo in Illinois. When a three-year-old boy fell into her enclosure in 1996, she carried him to safety.

WORDS to Know

antibodies   substances that destroy other disease-carrying substances

bushmeat   the meat of wild animals killed for food in tropical parts of the world

captivity   living in a place from which escape is not possible

deforestation   the clearing or thinning of forests by humans

endangered   at risk of dying out completely

hormones   chemical substances produced in the body that control the activity of certain cells and organs

mammals   animals that have a backbone and hair or fur, give birth to live young, and produce milk to feed their young

species   a group of living beings with shared characteristics and the ability to reproduce with one another

LEARN MORE

Books

Daly, Ruth. *Bringing Back the Mountain Gorilla.* New York: Crabtree, 2019.

Hodgson Meeker, Clare. *Growing Up Gorilla: How a Zoo Baby Brought Her Family Back Together.* Minneapolis: Millbrook Press, 2019.

Marsico, Katie. *Gorillas.* New York: Children's Press, 2017.

Websites

"All About Gorillas." The Ellen Fund. https://theellenfund.org/gorillas.

"Gorilla." San Diego Zoo Animals & Plants. https://animals.sandiegozoo.org /animals/gorilla.

"What Do Gorillas Eat? And Other Gorilla Facts." World Wildlife Fund. https://www.worldwildlife.org/stories/what-do-gorillas-eat-and-other -gorilla-facts.

Documentaries

Nikwigiza, Novella, and Lucas Rosenberg. *Saving Gorillas: Giving Nature a Voice.* Aga Khan University Graduate School of Media and Communications, 2017.

Tassier, Lydia. *In the Land of the Gorillas.* Owendo Productions, 2015.

Taylor, Jonathan. *Koko: The Gorilla Who Talks to People.* BBC, 2016.

Visit

CALGARY ZOO

Baby gorillas are born periodically through the zoo's gorilla conservation program.

210 St. George's Drive NE
Calgary, AB T2E 7V6
Canada

LOUISVILLE ZOO

Visitors can see gorillas and pygmy hippos up-close in a forested habitat.

1100 Trevilian Way
Louisville, KY 40213

SAN DIEGO ZOO SAFARI PARK

This 1,800-acre (728 ha) park is home to a family of western lowland gorillas.

15500 San Pasqual Valley Road
Escondido, CA 92027

ZOO ATLANTA

One of the largest groups of western lowland gorillas in North America lives at this zoo.

800 Cherokee Avenue SE
Atlanta, GA 30315

INDEX